Energy Wellness Blueprint

Energy Wellness Blueprint

Transform Your Stress, Reclaim Your Energy, and Increase Your Flow

KIMBERLY KINGSLEY

Copyright © 2025 by Kimberly Kingsley
Print Edition

All rights reserved.

Published in the United States by The Flow Lab, LLC
P.O. Box 4074, Scottsdale, Arizona 85261
TheFlowLab.co

Names: Kimberly Kingsley, author.

Title: Energy Wellness Blueprint: Transform Your Stress, Reclaim Your Energy, and Increase Your Flow.

Description: First Edition | Scottsdale, Arizona: The Flow Lab, LLC [2025] Subjects: Self-actualization (Psychology) | Flow | Mental health

Cover Design by Luis Medina
Edited by Kristine Nally
Formatted by Paul Salvette

For information about this title, contact the publisher: TheFlowLab.co

ISBN: 978-0-9964581-3-9

Contents

Introduction 1
    Not Self-Improvement 3

Chapter 1: Designed for Flow 5
    The Physics of Flow 7
    The Feeling of Flow 11
    Three Questions 14

Chapter 2: Personal Energy Flow 19
    Living in Reverse Flow 23
    The Language of Energy 25
    Catching Up with Yourself 28

Chapter 3: Energy Wellness Blueprint 31
    Your Giving Tree 33

Chapter 4: Presence—Your Roots 39
    Attention and Energy 41
    A Wider Bandwidth 42
    Time and Flow 46

Reclaiming Your Energy	48
Resistance to Presence	50
Intentional Breathing	52
Nourishing Environments	53
Practicing Presence	54
Reverse Flow Pathway	57
Treasure Hunt	61
Leveling Up	62
Chapter 5: Energy Integrity—Your Trunk	**65**
Energy Management	66
Vibe Tracker	69
Identifying Blind Spots	71
Karma	73
Emotional Flow	74
Thinking Pulls Us Out of Feeling	77
Emotional Whirlpools	79
Clarity and Conviction	81
Reverse Flow Pathway	82
Leveling Up	83
Chapter 6: Transformation—Your Branches	**87**
Flow Power	88
Taking Right Action	90
Flow Is Not Linear	92
Fast Flow and Slow Flow	93
Releasing Attachment	94

Staying Aligned in the Midst of Struggle	95
Reverse Flow Pathway	98
Reverse Flow Checklist	102
Untangling from Compensation Strategies	104
Leveling Up	105

Chapter 7: Flow—Your Fruit — 107

Sharing Your Energy with the World	108
Flow is Disruptive	110
Taking Mindful Risks	112
Passion and Purpose	116
Seeds are Delicate	119
Reflection: Assess Your Flow	121
Cultivating a Growth Mindset	127
Reverse Flow Pathway	129
Leveling Up	132
Celebrate Your Flow	134

Chapter 8: Living in Flow — 135

Acknowledgments — 149

Introduction

THE *ENERGY WELLNESS BLUEPRINT* is about living in your own flow. Something beautiful happens when we reclaim our energy and align with our flow. We become lighter and find ourselves naturally attuning to the world within and around us. We become "full of ourselves" in the best way possible. The feeling of missing something fades as we start to receive what we need instead of chasing the next best thing. We still get stressed but are less affected by the little things. More bounces off us and we experience greater resilience. At a point, when the energy within reaches our heart, we suddenly feel encouraged to do what we've known we needed to do for some time. Old patterns fall away and we disengage from low-level negativity and drama. We become keenly aware of the quality and quantity of energy we're experiencing in any given moment and quickly pivot when something doesn't feel nourishing or "high vibe." We develop a taste for fresh, positive energy and lose our appetite for stress energy, which starts to feel frenetic and ungrounded, like dirty electricity. When spontaneous right action arises without too much thought, you know you've entered into a dynamic dance with the ever-changing present moment we call flow. *When flow becomes a habit, we enter into an upward growth spiral that organically moves us toward our highest expression—the place where we both feel our best and do our best.*

Sadly, modern society doesn't support energy wellness, as the demands of everyday life encourage us to remain distracted and fragmented rather than present and whole. This causes our energy to splinter off in different directions, compromising our natural resilience and wellbeing. With so much competing for our attention, it's common to lose energy before it's had a chance to fill us up. This leaves us hungry and in search of what's missing—what's missing is our own energy and the inside-out fulfillment that flow brings. Social scientists refer to this as flourishing, which is the

Introduction

wellbeing that arises when we fully engage with life and direct our energy toward that which lights us up.

We've all had the experience of regaining our energy only to be flooded with ideas about how to express ourselves in new and creative ways. My firm belief is that prioritizing our energy is the fastest way to bring not only ourselves, but also the larger systems we inhabit, into greater harmony. This includes our relationships, workplaces, and society at large. Flow is the ultimate re-org: it buffs out what no longer works while taking us on an upward spiral that infuses us with energy and aligns us with our purpose.

Not Self-Improvement

Living in your flow is not about self-improvement, as you already have everything you need within you. We're not trying to get anywhere, find ourselves, or prove our worth. Nor are we trying to become enlightened, successful, or rich (although you'll definitely become lighter and will feel more successful). The goal, rather, is to step into and receive the stream of energy that's already there, allowing it to fill you up and inform your steps. We're designed for this, however, most of us need to untangle from that which drains our energy and diverts our flow. This is vital, as it's our energy that evolves us not our thinking. Once we reclaim our energy and manage it in a way that supports our flow, the insights and inspiration needed to move forward will naturally arise and move us toward right action. Remaining in alignment (and the willingness to return when we inevitably fall out) is all that's required to experience true energy wellness.

1

Designed for Flow

LIFE IS LIKE WALKING A TIGHTROPE. When we get it right, it feels effortless—like magic. But if we get too tense on one hand, or too relaxed on the other, we lose our balance and can't even take one step. Collectively we've lost our balance, vacillating between extreme stress and zoning out, neither of which provide the quality of energy that we crave. Stress pinches off flow while zoning out leads to the opposite extreme where we're no longer in command of our energy and attention.

You are designed for flow. If you think about it, any time you're flowing, whether talking to a friend or working on something you love, you feel happy, almost exhilarated. Why does flow feel so good? It's nature's way of rewarding us for sharing our energy with the world. In flow, a cascade of neurochemicals flood the body, helping us maintain our focus and continue moving in the right direction. What is it that's moving in a state of flow? Energy. *We are happiest when we direct our energy toward meaningful connection, creativity, and contribution.* When we focus our attention on what matters most, an integrated stream of energy flows from the inside out, filling us up prior to extending into the world.

It's no wonder flow is so addictive. Athletes know this, as do many others who've reached a level of mastery that allows them to enter flow at will. Peak performance, however, is only one stage of flow—it's the majestic waterfall at the end of a long and winding river. Before the waterfall can take our breath away, rainwater, streams, and tributaries must gather into a single flow channel with enough power to literally move mountains. Stepping into our flow is how we align with the river of energy moving through us so that we can show up as the force of nature we came here to be and "move mountains" in our own life.

Some of the highest performing and emotionally intelligent people I know are stuck in "overdrive," a state of chronic stress that's hard to get out of. This is understandable, as the speed and unpredictability of life has become a lot to process even for the most agile among us. While we may not be able to control what's going on in the world, we can control where we direct our energy and attention. This is key, as once our nervous system shifts out of overdrive, the energy within can resume its job of guiding us forward, where the feeling in your gut, the tingle on your skin, and the deep knowing you can't explain takes the place of circular thinking and constant fact finding.

The Physics of Flow

Far from woo-woo, flow is nature's blueprint and life's design. We see this design throughout the natural world. If you imagine the earth from space, you'll see a circulatory system of interconnected veins of water that feed her land and maintain the abundant life on this planet. We too are comprised of layers and layers of flow systems that serve to keep us healthy and brimming with life. We have blood flow, oxygen flow, and digestive flow. Information flows from our nervous system to our brain and back again, allowing our body to maintain homeostasis despite a constantly changing environment. In addition to the flow systems that are seen, there are many that are unseen. Energy flow is one such system. Emotional flow, relationship flow, and creative flow are just some of the ways that energy "moves" us, extending through our body and into the world.

In physics, this universal flow design is known as the *constructal law*. Adrian Bejan of Duke University fathered this law and has been gracious enough to help me understand it from a lay person's perspective. In his book, *The Physics of Life*, Bejan describes this law: "For a flow system to persist in time (to live) it must evolve freely such that it provides greater access to its currents."[1] I've had several conversations with Professor

---

[1] Bejan, Adrian. *The Physics of Life: The Evolution of Everything.* New York, NY: St. Martin's Press, 2016, 239.

Bejan as well as the opportunity to interview him on my podcast, *High Vibrational Life*. Here, we apply this universal design in nature to our personal energy so that we can increase flow (and therefore, wellbeing and purpose) in every area of our life.

Learning about the constructal law confirmed what I intuited in my twenties after experiencing a radical realignment of my own energy flow. After a period of intense anxiety, something shifted, and instead of frantically searching for energy outside myself, my energy began flowing from the inside out. The relief I experienced was profound. But along with relief there was grief. Why hadn't anyone taught me how to be a healthy human? Why did I have to spend so much time anxious and confused? The truth is that the adults in my life, as wonderful as they were, didn't know either—at least not in a way that they could describe. This fueled my desire to learn more, as only when I slowed down enough to reconnect with the stream of energy moving through me did my anxiety start to dissipate. In flow, I finally found peace.

While I don't pretend to understand physics, I do understand the human psyche and how we thrive. As a counselor and energy coach, I've had the privilege of witnessing countless people reclaim their energy and return to their flow. Everyone's journey is unique but one thing is for sure: fully stepping into your own flow is the most courageous choice you will ever make. It's the real hero's journey and the ultimate act of bravery. It can be scary to prioritize our flow after years and decades of pouring energy into the same habits, relationships, and thought patterns, but when we slow down enough to feel what's real, we know what is and isn't flowing in our lives. What if we just need to trust ourselves enough to live according to our inner knowing? Remembering that we're designed for flow takes the guilt out of being true to ourselves. The reality is that the highest form of service is showing up as an authentically positive presence. An empty gesture serves no one, but one energized and heartfelt "hello" can transform someone's day.

The Feeling of Flow

This brings us to a very important point about the physics of personal energy flow: there are times when flow feels anything but flowy. Sometimes the energy moving through us feels exhilarating and other times it feels heavy or even stagnant. This is especially true when we're dealing with grief, recovering from an illness, or in the midst of a big change—there are times when we're simply exhausted and need to go slow.

For obvious reasons, most of us gravitate more toward the high side of flow. Being in love is a good example. When we're "in love," energy rushes through us so fast that we can hardly contain ourselves, often bubbling over into laughter or a spontaneous kiss. It's common to think it's the other person, but the feeling of being in love is really the velocity of energy moving through your body and opening your heart center. When we mistakenly think our love is dependent upon one specific person, we unfairly make them responsible for the joy that arises in response to abundant inner flow.

Peak performance and time in the zone is another example of the high side of flow. Whether working on a passion project or crushing a workout, time in the zone elevates us out of the mundane and creates an almost instantaneous feedback loop in which everything seems to fall into place. The feeling is so intoxicating that it can be addictive. However, many brilliant and high performing people have emotionally and physically imploded as a result of becoming addicted to the high side of flow. While drugs, alcohol, and reckless risk taking might seem like a short-cut to flow, the secret to more time in the zone is renewal and replenishing our neurochemistry. Everyone, no matter how accomplished or brilliant, ebbs *and* flows and embracing the ebb is how we support our flow.

Ebbs and flows are part of the language of energy that we're all learning to speak. We can and should experience the highs of flow, but if we fail to honor the ebbs or try to avoid the choppy waters of heavier and more "negative" emotions, the energy intended to evolve us will get blocked and become harder to access. Sometimes our awareness decides to jump ship rather than stay steady amidst the choppy currents of stress, anxiety, or frustration, but that which we seek to avoid is often the pressure of unprocessed energy knocking at the door asking to be let in.

These uncertain times make it especially important to honor the ebb side of flow, as just like a mature tree is able withstand major storms, we too, experience tremendous resilience when we remain anchored in our body and connected to our flow. When we honor the energy within, however it presents itself, life begins to feel more like a string of flow experiences that vary in intensity rather than the extreme highs and lows of peak performance and exhaustion. When floating down a river, most of us enjoy the mellow currents as much as the exciting rapids.

Inner flow leads to outer flow and to experience true energy wellness, we need both. This book explores an approach to personal energy management that aligns us with the fundamental truth that we can't give what we don't have and that we don't have to live in a state of chronic stress to thrive and achieve our purpose. There is an alternative—one that promotes both wellbeing and purpose—and that alternative is flow.

Three Questions

Your level of energy wellness determines how you feel, how you show up, and the extent to which you experience meaning and purpose in your life. The following three questions are designed to help you reflect on your current level of energy wellness. I recommend writing the answers down so that you can refer back to them in the future and see how things change as you increase your energy wellness and flow.

- *How do I feel?*
- *How do I show up?*
- *Do I live on purpose?*

How do I feel (energy and mood) most of the time?

The first question, "How do I feel?" relates to your energy and mood. The goal isn't to be in a great mood all the time as everyone has bad days, it's more about how you feel *most* of the time. Do you experience an overall lightness of being? Are you able to shake things off pretty easily? Or, do you feel stressed all the time and spend too much time in your head thinking and worrying about things that you can't control. As you explore this first question, it's important not to judge or analyze your experience. Just tune into the feeling of being you in this current phase of your life.

How do I show up? (What quality of energy do I bring to others?)

The second question, "How do I show up?" relates to how others perceive you. Energy is contagious and we affect the people around us more than we know. The quality of energy that we bring to a situation has the power to either elevate others or bring them down. When we take responsibility for our personal energy, our presence literally becomes a gift. On the flip side, if we're always stressed or irritated, we may be infecting others without even knowing it. Like your mood, how you show up varies day by day, so consider how you show up *most of the time*.

Do I live my life on purpose and with present-moment intentionality?

The third question relates to how you manage and direct your energy. In flow, purpose becomes a path rather than a destination. Without a pathway, a river would never make it to the ocean. Sometimes we have a sense of our bigger purpose and sometimes we don't, but when we remain connected to the stream of energy moving through us, the next right action opens up before us. Purpose in this sense is both micro and macro. Micro purpose is about present-moment intentionality and doing the next right thing, while macro purpose relates to the unique way that we share our gifts with the world. As you reflect on this question, consider the level of fulfillment or satisfaction that you experience most days in response to how you direct your energy—remembering that everyone has an occasional chaotic or unproductive day, and that perfection is the enemy of flow.

Perfection is the enemy of flow.

2

Personal Energy Flow

YOU ARE A FLOW SYSTEM just like the ones found in nature—energy is the current and the landscape is you: your body, mind, and life. When open and aligned on the inside, each moment brings fresh energy into our awareness as information and inspiration—information "informs" our choices, while inspiration "moves" us toward right action. The information embedded in energy presents itself as feelings, instincts, intuition, sensations, and hunches, helping us to navigate our lives with awareness and ease.

It's easy to see ourselves as fixed, but in reality, we are highly fluid beings who continuously change and evolve with our environment. When a river flows through a landscape, for example, both the water and landscape are changed. The water changes as it picks up minerals and debris from the landscape, while the landscape is shaped by the water flowing through it. This is true for us as well—as energy moves through us, we are shaped by it, continuously being in-formed, re-formed, and over time, trans-formed. Then, depending on how we choose to direct our energy, we shape the various landscapes of our lives including our relationships, careers, and passions.

Many things in today's world pull us out of our flow. This happens when we fall into over-thinking or get sucked into social media and lose track of time. But even when our awareness jumps ship, our nervous system still does its job of picking up energy and information from the environment. Missing too many moments in a row causes energy to build up within our body and nervous system where it waits for us to return to a state of presence so that it can be processed through our mind/body flow channel. Neglecting to process life as it occurs adds to the burden of unprocessed emotion that many people carry from past challenges that were too much to process at the time. Many, if not most, of us are walking around with a backlog of unprocessed energy that feels like stress or the sense of being overwhelmed. You can imagine this build-up of energy as water behind a cracking dam. The longer we ignore it, the more intense it gets, often turning into chronic stress or anxiety. We might find ourselves stuck in whirlpools of repeating thoughts and corresponding emotions as our mind unconsciously tries to resolve our distress.

Any unprocessed energy consumes a portion of our bandwidth much like an app that's running on your phone even when it's not being used. This silently drains our battery and adds to the feeling of stress and overwhelm. I once heard mindfulness teacher Tara Brach describe the feeling of overwhelm as having multiple tabs open in your mind at the same time. This is exactly how it feels. We can become so overwhelmed that we are "driven to distraction" as form of escape. Distraction is the ultimate trickster because it offers temporary relief in the form of dopamine while simultaneously diverting more energy away from our flow channel.

In addition to escaping into distraction, we might start chasing energy in the form of stress hormones (cortisol and adrenalin) generated through rushing, worrying, and stressing ourselves out over little things. Just as a child prefers negative attention over no attention, many people prefer "stress energy" to low energy. Some people are so dependent on stress energy that they don't know how they'd function without it. If you're wondering if you fall into this category, just ask yourself how often you feel stressed. If the answer is "very often" then there's a good chance that you're relying on stress hormones to fuel your day instead of regularly dipping into the well of fresh energy available to us in presence.

Your Relationship with Stress

Moving into greater flow involves taking an honest look at our relationship with stress. Is it a healthy relationship? Relying on stress energy to get through the day sets us up for anxiety, burnout and countless stress-related illnesses. It's not that all stress is bad—stress hormones are there to help us survive and thrive. The kind of stress that's most concerning is chronic stress, which leads to the over-production of cortisol. Living in a state of chronic stress is very different than experiencing acute stress in times of danger, or even eustress, which is the positive stress experienced when we push ourselves beyond our comfort zone, as when giving a talk or taking a surfing lesson. Disrupting chronic stress is essential for living a life that flows, and for many of us, stress has become a habit rather than a survival mechanism.

Living in Reverse Flow

When dopamine-driven distraction and stress-generating behaviors become habitual we can flip into a type of *reverse flow,* which is an orientation to life that involves chasing energy instead of receiving it as we're designed. Reverse flow feels like living on a hamster wheel. Instead of slowing down to process what's there, we grab a snack, scroll on our phones, or rush to run an errand. But as we know and have experienced a hundred times, mindless consumption and aimless activity never fills us up, despite the momentary sense of pleasure or relief that it brings. You may have noticed that scrolling on your phone, for example, provides a short-term boost but quickly turns into a drain. It's not that we need to avoid these things altogether. It's more about the intention driving the behavior and the impact that it has on our energy. In flow, all of life's pleasures become even more pleasurable. Energized from the inside-out, we engage with whatever we're doing from a place of fullness instead of looking for a person, place, or thing to fill us up. And even when we do find ourselves chasing energy in the form of cheap dopamine or stress hormones, it's no problem, as everyone moves in and out of flow all the time.

Stress Culture

It's worth noting that our habits—even the seemingly negative or unproductive ones—are there to help us cope. In addition to the very real stressors that we've faced in recent years, most of us have grown up in what could be described as *stress culture*—a society that glorifies reverse flow and, now more than ever, capitalizes on our attention, energy, and over-consumption. Viewing our habits through this wider lens mitigates toxic shame and makes it easier to untangle from the various systems designed to capture our attention and energy. Taking full responsibility for our energy is one of the most impactful forms of protest—what we don't feed must transform. Simply ask yourself, who and what do I wish to feed? My guess is that you wish to feed *your* purpose and creative pursuits.

The Language of Energy

Just as naming our feelings helps us to process them, specifically describing our energy empowers us to manage it in a way that supports our flow. *Reverse flow*, for example, describes the feeling of chasing energy but never feeling fulfilled or satisfied. Rather than sustain us, reverse flow behaviors deplete our neurochemistry and lower our resilience. I refer to this type of energy as *stress energy* because, while it might provide a short-term boost, reverse flow doesn't fuel or nourish us. Throughout this book, I'll use the term *stress energy* to describe energy that's generated through stress hormones and cheap dopamine versus fresh energy that's received and channeled in a way that supports our wellbeing and flow.

I'll use the terms *flow channel* and *mind/body flow channel* to describe you as a container through which energy flows, and *flow* to describe the current of energy moving through you. And because nature is our best teacher, I'll be using both river and tree metaphors to describe personal energy flow, as these natural wonders have a lot to teach us about managing our energy in a way that promotes wellbeing, growth, and flow.

Two Pathways

As we move through each step of the Blueprint, you'll notice that two pathways emerge—one path takes you on an upward growth spiral that enhances your wellbeing and flow, while the other takes you further and further away from your flow, resulting in the progressive need to compensate through reverse flow behaviors. Just as there are stages of personal energy flow, there are stages of reverse flow. Clearly identifying the stages of reverse flow help us maintain our alignment and make choices that promote energy wellness instead of stress.

Catching Up with Yourself

We are constantly changing and evolving, but sometimes we get stuck on an old lens that no longer reflects who we've become. Holding on to an outdated version of ourselves such as the ten-year-old self who was painfully shy or the teenager who was "always into trouble" keeps us tethered to a time that has long since passed. The truth is that you're not even the same version of yourself that you were yesterday let alone when you were ten.

When we hold on to an outdated identity, we spread our energy over the landscape of our life and dilute our power in the present. Releasing redundant self-concepts allows us to reclaim our energy from the past and lighten our load in the present. This creates space for the aspects of you that are ready and waiting to burst forth.

The following questions invite you to "catch up with yourself" by releasing what's no longer needed and coming fully into the present where you're able to receive and birth the version of you that's waiting to emerge. Again, it's best to write the answers down in your notebook or journal so that you can reflect back on them later.

1. Are you holding on to an image, identity, or concept of yourself that is no longer relevant? Where did it come from? How does it hold you back?

2. What gifts, lessons, or protection did you receive from this old image, identity, or belief? In other words, how did it serve you?

3. If you're ready to let it go, thank this previous version of yourself for its gifts/lessons and gently release it into the stream of energy moving through you.

4. Can you sense a version of yourself that is ready and waiting to emerge? If so, describe it in your notebook or journal.

5. What actions can you take to embody this fresh version of you?

Energy Wellness Blueprint

NATURE MAKES NO MISTAKES. She designed us to grow, thrive, and flow—to blossom into our full expression for the purpose of generously sharing our gifts. To do this, we need to move into alignment with our natural flow design and receive the stream of energy moving through us. The *Energy Wellness Blueprint* is a four-step process that mirrors the stages of flow in nature and aligns us with our natural way of being. Each stage in the process brings your energy to the next level so that it fills you up prior to extending into the world—we can't help but give back when we're overflowing. This is nature's way.

The four steps to energy wellness are Presence, Energy Integrity, Transformation, and Flow. *Presence* is how we connect and receive energy. *Energy Integrity* is how we manage and integrate the energy we receive—nature's integrity is structural rather than moral and no different from the structural integrity of a river bed or the structural integrity of a tree trunk—without boundaries there is no flow. *Transformation* is the change and growth that occurs when we apply our energy in line with our inner knowing. And *Flow*—the final step—is how we give back and express our energy in new and unique ways. Flow is the sacred meeting place between inner and outer and where giving and receiving become one, as when we offer our gifts from a place of fullness, we are fulfilled.

Picture each step stacked on top of one another like a tree with roots, a trunk, branches, and fruit—it is this stacking or *alignment* that enables flow. You are a giving tree—not the kind that gives everything until you're just a stump on the ground, but an elegant flow system that gives generously because you have more than enough to share. Presence is your roots, Energy Integrity is your trunk, Transformation is your branches, and Flow is your fruit. Everything pales in comparison to the feeling of living in your own flow and sharing from this place of natural abundance.

Your Giving Tree

Before we go deeper into each step, it will be helpful to get a visual representation of your flow. After reading the descriptions below, draw a tree that represents you as a flow system. I encourage you to put a reminder on your calendar to draw another tree in six months. I predict that in the coming months, your roots will grow stronger and more energy will be flowing through your trunk (mind/body flow channel). This will result in the growth and strengthening of some of the branches in your life and the falling away of others as your inner and outer world reorganize to accommodate your increased flow.

Your Roots

The roots of your tree represent your level of presence and the extent to which you connect with yourself and others for the purpose of *receiving*. In presence, we receive energy and information through our senses and nervous system, which, not surprisingly, resembles the roots of a tree. We bring in fresh energy from within and around us and release that which is no longer needed. This prevents stagnant energy from accumulating in our body and allows us to continuously renew.

As you reflect on the strength and size of your roots, consider the following questions: Do you take time to connect with yourself daily in stillness? Do you regularly release stress and discharge accumulated energy? Are you planted in nourishing environments? Do you give others the attention they deserve? Are you a good listener? If you answered yes to these questions, your roots will be deep and strongly anchored in the present. If you, like many people, find yourself frequently distracted and only give yourself and others fleeting or partial attention, your roots will be smaller and shallower, affecting your ability to receive the full bandwidth of energy and information available to you each moment.

Your Trunk

The trunk of your tree represents Energy Integrity and the extent to which you experience healthy inner flow as opposed to emotional suppression, energy congestion, and chronic stress. Integrating and protecting our energy provides the information and inspiration needed to move forward and creates a strong and integrated channel through which energy can flow. Alternatively, fragmented and mismanaged energy weakens our trunk, lowers our resilience, and diminishes our capacity for inner and outer flow.

Some questions to consider when drawing your trunk: Do you identify and process (feel) emotions as they arise? Do you manage your energy in a way that reduces unnecessary stress? Are you able to say "no" when necessary to protect your energy resources? Are you present with your emotions without suppressing or exploding? Do you trust the information (feelings, sensations, instincts, insights) you receive and allow this knowing to inform your choices?

If you answered yes to the above questions, your trunk will be strong and clear enough to process the real-time flow of energy and information. If, on the other hand, you routinely suppress your feelings or release emotions impulsively, your trunk might be small, have holes in it, or perhaps even be bloated from carrying a backlog of unprocessed energy. If you're in the habit of silencing yourself rather than expressing your thoughts, feelings, and needs, your trunk may look more like an hourglass than a tree. Consistently losing energy through distraction or self-sabotaging behaviors might be illustrated by a fragile or broken trunk or your trunk might be shorter than you'd like and unable to reach new heights.

Your Branches

The branches of your tree represent Transformation—the natural change and growth that takes place when we apply our energy with integrity (according to our inner knowing). Your branches also illustrate all the ways that you extend yourself into the world. This includes your relationships, work, hobbies, and habits. When we avoid or delay doing what we know need to do, our energy stagnates as do the branches of our lives.

When drawing your branches, consider both the strength and health of each branch and the extent to which energy is flowing in that area of your life. You might draw a branch for each important relationship in your life along with branches to represent your work, hobbies, habits, and passions. When it comes to the size and strength of each branch, consider the actions you take and whether you trust yourself enough to do what's right. You might notice that you're carrying dead weight in the form of branches that no longer flow or support your growth. Ask yourself, "Am I willing to release that which is ready to fall away in order to make room for new growth? If a certain branch isn't growing the way that you'd like, you might ask yourself, "What am I avoiding?" We can delay right action for a time, but long-term avoidance usually results in forced transformation, during which nature steps in and takes over, costing more energy and heartache in the long run. On the other hand, we strengthen and grow new branches every time we act in alignment with our inner knowing, learn a new skill, or communicate with integrity and courage. You might notice that some of your branches are thriving while others are struggling. How does this imbalance affect you as a whole?

Your Fruit

The fruit of your tree represents Flow and the extent to which you share your gifts and presence with the world. We cannot underestimate the power of our presence once our energy reaches this level—in flow, your presence truly becomes a gift. Even when you're having a bad day, you'll still emanate positivity because your energy is flowing.

When drawing the fruit of your tree, consider the extent to which you share your gifts with the world. You might ask yourself, "Do I take mindful risks and put myself out there enough?" "Am I willing to fail?" "Do I feel fulfilled?" "Does my life have meaning?" "Am I generous with my time and energy?" Keep in mind that we can't give what we don't have, so if you are not able to answer yes to some of these questions, it may be that you are losing energy in one of the first three stages. Once you regain your energy, you will have the information and inspiration needed to move forward, and the fruits of your labor will become evident. If you answered yes to the above questions, you are doing a good job managing your energy in a way that supports your wellbeing and growth—congratulations, you are flowing.

4

Presence—Your Roots

PRESENCE IS THE FIRST STEP in the *Energy Wellness Blueprint* and brings us into alignment with the flow of energy moving through us. Acting as our roots, presence plants us firmly in our body and allows us to receive fresh energy and information from within and around us. And because energy wellness comes from processing life as it occurs, presence prevents stress and the build-up of energy congestion. In addition to cultivating a daily presence practice, we use *energy awareness* and *attention management* to stay connected and present throughout the day.

Presence is both a location and a frequency—take a moment and let that sink in. Being present involves bringing your full awareness into the space that you're in, while your "presence" is the quality of energy that you bring into that space—your vibe. When we show up partially present, our presence is diminished, but when we show up to a space fully present, our presence is felt—we have a powerful presence.

Presence initiates flow by activating our ability to connect and receive. The moment we become present to something or someone, energy floods into our awareness, providing information about whatever we are tuning into. Even walking by a stranger can initiate the flow of energy and information. Our antenna goes up and we immediately know all kinds of things about them, whether they are successful or struggling, happy or sad, etc. Depending on your level of sensitivity, you might pick up on more than that as well. Presence is also activated on the giving side of the flow channel (the fourth step), however, step one is about receiving energy, as without a current, there is no flow.

Attention and Energy

Attention is how we manage our presence and energy on both ends of the flow channel—receiving and giving. For example, you can be present and focused or present and relaxed. Focused attention acts like a two-way plug in a wall socket—it initiates the exchange of energy and information. If we resonate with someone or something, the exchange will be fluid and we'll feel uplifted and inspired. However, if we pay too much attention to things that bring us down, we can become "infected" with sticky, low vibrational energy. We often mistake this sticky energy for our own, assuming that we're just "stressed" or in a bad mood. With awareness and practice we can start to identify what is and isn't ours and quickly release any heavy energies that we pick up along the way.

Managing our attention is one of the most effective ways to prevent stress and promote overall energy wellness. Just as we're mindful about energy use in our home, we can use our attention to manage the input and output of our personal energy. One simple strategy is to alternate between focused attention (convergent focus), which is neurochemically demanding, and expanded awareness (divergent focus) which allows us to unwind and replenish. Picking up your phone to relax is counterproductive because visually focusing on a screen still requires focused attention, and while you may *feel* more relaxed, your brain still needs to produce focus chemicals (norepinephrine), and therefore your nervous system won't be able to fully unwind. The ability to manage one's attention is a superpower that few possess. Consistently flexing our attention muscle by shifting our awareness at will puts us in the driver's seat of our own life—we get to choose who and what we connect with and when to unplug and renew.

A Wider Bandwidth

Awareness is the part of us that's bigger than both our attention and energy. Awareness allows us to observe how we're using our attention and where our energy is flowing. Energy Awareness, or more specifically, embodied awareness—staying connected to your body and nervous system (inner roots)—is one of the most important skills of our time because it anchors us in the here and now even as life continues to accelerate around us.

Being embodied takes us out of our head (which has only a limited view of reality—a mental view with many filters and distortions) and enables us to receive information on four distinct wavelengths: physical, emotional, mental, and spiritual or energetic. This increased bandwidth means that our body often knows things before our brain has had a chance to register what's happening. This is called bottom-up processing. For example, you might get a pit in your stomach when you meet someone while at the same time your brain is telling you to give them a chance. *Energy never lies* but it's our job to pay attention to the information we receive. When energy awareness becomes a habit, we learn to trust the signals within and around us and steer our lives accordingly. The ability to process life as it occurs makes us extremely agile. Like a river, we weave in and out of our day with purpose and direction, moving gracefully around boulders and flowing right on by energy-consuming whirlpools.

Most of us practice energy awareness without even thinking, but in this rapidly changing world, it's worth taking this skill up a notch. Practicing energy awareness allows us to be selective about what (and who) we tune into, as whatever energies we ingest, we must also digest. Just as we choose what foods to eat, we can and should be selective about what energies we invite into our flow channel—especially when it comes to technology and social media platforms that are designed to get (and keep) our attention. When we connect with something that's negative or low vibrational, we not only bring that energy into our flow channel but we also feed it our energy and support its growth. Equally as important as our ability to connect with the outside world is our ability to disconnect. We can do this quickly and efficiently by shifting our focus and moving on.

Shifting the Vibe

How do we deal with "negative" vibes? Do we walk away or politely excuse ourselves? Sometimes it might be necessary to excuse ourselves, but often we can shift the vibe of a conversation by being aware of the *whole person* that's in front of us rather than hyper-focusing on the pattern that's activated within them. When we can be there for others in the right way—present and open—we support them to return to alignment and process whatever they're carrying. Most people will respond well to our openness and positive intentions. However, if a person is a chronic complainer or energy vampire, feeding that pattern with our attention and energy is not helpful for them and invites that quality of energy into our flow channel. Regardless of whether we're engaging with people, social media, or our own thinking, being selective about where we place our attention is like eating a clean diet—it's less for us to process on an energetic level and keeps us clear on the inside.

Resonance versus Reason

When it comes to energy, resonance trumps reason. If you don't resonate or feel the integrity of someone you're tuning into, it's important to trust that and flow on by. You can feel when someone is living in integrity and powered by a love frequency. A love frequency is a like a symphony—a synthesis of physical, emotional, mental, and spiritual energies that are expressed in a congruent way. An integral person powered by harmonized energy feels very different than someone who's fragmented on the inside and leading with a persona. It's imperative in today's world that we perceive beyond the limited bandwidth of mentalization and reason. Being present and aligned gives us a much bigger picture than thoughts alone.

Time and Flow

We often hear that time doesn't really exist, but if we reframe time as the flow of energy and information, then it certainly does exist and is the only thing that we truly have the power to influence. Our relationship with time changes when we're aligned and in our flow. We realize the futility of procrastination and minimize the delay between knowing and acting—when a wave hits, we ride it by acting on the information we receive as soon as possible. This morning, I felt the inner nudge to call my cousin. I rarely make calls in the morning because it's my most productive writing time. Nevertheless, I followed my urge to pick up the phone and call her. As soon as she heard my voice, she shared that her mom had taken a turn for the worse and was going into hospice. Had I ignored or delayed the inner nudge, I wouldn't have known about my aunt until much later.

Acting on our inner knowing keeps us open on the inside and the waves of inspiration start coming faster. Trusting our flow isn't something we learn, it is something we practice. The more connected we are to ourselves and the full bandwidth of our reality, the clearer and louder these inner impulses become. I was recently talking to someone who said, "I feel like time is moving so fast, but I'm not getting anywhere." I asked her what she was doing when she had this insight and she said she was watching Instagram Shorts. It occurred to me how many of us unknowingly distract ourselves while life (the real-time flow of energy and information) flows right on by.

Where do we go when we step out of the full bandwidth (physical, emotional, mental, and spiritual) of our awareness? To be clear, we don't go anywhere, but it is possible to limit our perception to a mere sliver of reality such as when we get stuck in our head (mental time) or hyper-focus on technology (technology time). It's as if our awareness gets sucked into a vortex and we lose touch with the broader signals trying to get our attention. Practicing embodied awareness keeps us connected and in our flow. Had my friend been aware of her body, she would have known to get off her phone—our body tells us loud and clear when we're losing energy and time is "passing us by."

Reclaiming Your Energy

A side effect of living in the attention economy is that our energy has become strung out, fragmented, and buried. We've scattered this precious current across the landscape of our lives, locked it in our body, and given it away to others. Every time we're fully present, however, we make space for a fragmented piece of our energy to integrate back into our awareness. We've all had the experience of becoming still only to receive a wave of love, gratitude, or sadness that we didn't even know was there. Insights can hit us from seemingly out of nowhere. This is why it's so important to *practice presence*, as this is how we become wholly integrated—presence heals us by making us whole. In addition to making us whole, presence transforms us into a positive presence or someone who has *good vibes*.

Shamanic traditions refer to the process of reclaiming our energy as recapitulation—the recapturing of oneself. Reclaiming our energy is essential for returning to our flow. The good news is that being present is as natural as breathing. We just need to turn our lens inward and allow the light of our awareness to strengthen our roots and increase our capacity to receive.

Resistance to Presence

Many people experience a subtle resistance to presence. This is understandable, as our fast-paced life makes it difficult to process events in real-time, which leads to a backlog of emotional energy that can feel overwhelming to tune into. Adding to the hum of overwhelm is the chronic stress that many, many people are experiencing. The combination of unprocessed energy and unrelenting stress makes it hard to get out of our head and drop into presence.

We can ease into presence by expanding our awareness beyond our thoughts. Less mental activity helps our nervous system slowly transition out of stress energy (cortisol and adrenalin) and into a more grounded and balanced energy. The more we unwind, the easier it is to become present. An example of this is going on vacation and finding that it takes two or three days to completely relax. Slowing down and becoming present can sometimes trigger an initial energy lull or period of exhaustion, especially when one is coming out of an extended period of stress or teetering on burn-out. Exhaustion, while not pleasant, is a type of recovery and can be viewed as an opportunity for renewal. We all know what happens when we ignore our body for too long—eventually, nature takes over and forces us to rest, often in response to a mental or physical illness.

Both movement and time in nature accelerate renewal. Movement helps us process stress hormones and move into a more expansive energy, while being in nature grounds us and helps us to get out of our head. Mounting evidence suggests that activities such as forest bathing soothe our nervous system and enhance our mood. My experience is that nature brings us into alignment perhaps faster than anything else. Alignment initiates rapid processing and integration, as once all the levels of self (physical, emotional, mental, spiritual) align and start communicating, our energy begins to flow and we become aware of that which was previously hidden. For this reason, being in nature is like therapy—it helps us release whatever it is we're carrying and renews us from the inside-out. We can bring this enhanced alignment into every setting by practicing embodied awareness and making sure that no part of us is running ahead (mental sprinting) or lagging behind (suppressed emotions).

Intentional Breathing

Breathwork of all kinds has exploded in popularity and for good reason, it's one of the few ways to directly influence our nervous system and improve our emotional state. Just as managing our attention is key for managing our energy, intentional breathing promotes either a sympathetic (energizing) or parasympathetic (calming) response from our nervous system. As a general rule, extended exhalations discharge stress and calm our energy, while extended inhalations increase energy and promote heightened focus. Rhythmic breathing—inhaling and exhaling for equal amounts of time—is ideal for balancing our energy and regulating our nervous system. When we're connected to our roots and practicing embodied awareness, we know when we're becoming stressed or if our energy starts to dip. Here's the hack—when you're stressed, calm your breathing and extend your exhale slightly. When your energy is low and focus is waning, extend your inhales and bring more oxygen into your body. Managing our energy in real-time is the ultimate form of stress prevention, and intentional breathing is something we can do anytime and anywhere.

Nourishing Environments

Nature thrives in nourishing environments, and we too, need to plant ourselves in nourishing environments to grow our roots and flourish. This includes home, work, and friendships. What is a nourishing environment? It is simply one in which we feel safe enough to be ourselves. Organizations refer to this as psychological safety. In every environment, there will be a mix of energies that include hard times, good times, and periods of uncertainty. Unsafe or toxic environments are different—rather than natural ups and downs, these environments are unpredictable, volatile, and sometimes even hostile. The lack of predictability activates the protective and defensive parts of us while the more authentic and vulnerable parts go underground. When we're forced to hide and compartmentalize our inner world, our energy can't flow and our nervous system (our roots) will be stuck in fight or flight. This is why stress makes us sick.

We've all worked and lived in unsafe environments, at least most of us have, and getting out of these environments can take time. The first stage of flow—Presence—allows us to feel what's real without distracting ourselves. If we remain present and alert to the signals in our body, our energy will guide us to take the next right step. Everyone deserves to live and work in nourishing environments and the most integrated among us will not be able to tolerate anything less. This hard boundary is exceedingly positive and how we protect our flow.

Practicing Presence

As a society, we've become so outer focused that our roots have atrophied. This makes it harder to *receive* the nourishing energy we crave. Practicing presence for as little as ten minutes a day regrows our roots and strengthens our ability to receive energy and information from within. Your primary relationship is with you. Just as being present to someone you love nourishes your bond, being present to yourself strengthens your relationship with yourself. This is how we give our heart and gut a voice and prevent our mind from micromanaging our life.

Something rarely considered is that *presence requires energy*. I'm sure you can relate to the feeling of being so depleted that you don't have the energy to listen to someone who's trying to talk to you. Being present is energetically demanding, and having a regular presence practice fortifies our ability to connect with others and *receive* them.

If you're one of the many people who feel overwhelmed by the idea of meditation, you can start by practicing several minutes of embodied awareness each day. This involves expanding your awareness to include your entire body while mindfully breathing at a pace that feels natural. It's that simple. There are a hundred ways to practice presence and all of them are correct. If your mind starts racing whenever you become still, visualization can help. Next time you practice presence, try imagining your energy filling you up the way water fills a cup. Water represents your energy. Start by taking a few mindful breaths, as our breath is an anchor in meditation and in life. After anchoring into your body with a few mindful breaths, bring your awareness to your feet and imagine water filling you up from the tips of your toes all the way to the top of your head. Try sitting a minute or two longer than you'd like, as we often experience the urge to stop when our energy reaches a block. For example, you might feel the urge to get up when you feel the energy has reached your stomach. But what if you wait until it reaches your heart? Or your throat? What you'll find is that the more energy you're able to receive and absorb, the more resilience you'll have throughout the day.

If nothing else, we can practice what I call *Wake to Flow*. Wake to flow involves spending the first few moments of your waking day in a receptive state. This doesn't take long—just a couple of minutes of expanded awareness fills you with fresh energy and often brings insights on the heels of the extended period of rest. Your mind will want to start racing the moment you wake up, but if we immediately start planning our day or get on our phone, we lose the magic window upon waking when our brain is still in a receptive alpha state.

Maintaining Positive Energy

We can maintain our positive energy (flowing energy) throughout the day by taking periodic "brain breaks." Simply taking a few slow, deep breaths between tasks helps quiet the mind and make space for bottom-up processing. Our brain tells our body what to do all day; it's important to give our body a chance to communicate as well. With so much stimuli coming our way, it's easy to ignore our body and the information that it's trying to share. But suppressing our inner world while bringing in a near-constant stream of input adds to whatever backlog we're already carrying. Creating space for bottom-up processing keeps us open, aligned, and in our flow.

Reverse Flow Pathway

Distraction is the first stage of the reverse flow pathway. We become distracted when something captures our attention and causes our energy to start flowing in another direction. You may have heard the saying, *where attention goes, energy flows*. This is absolutely true and the reason why guarding our attention is paramount.

Distractions can come from within or be triggered by our environment. Screens are an obvious culprit, as they seem to hold the promise of something more exciting than the moment that we're in. But a more insidious and often overlooked distraction is our own thinking, which can take the form mindless looping, or even a *thought virus*, which is an intrusive thought or negative belief that seems to take on a life of its own. We catch these thought viruses from society and other people and then feed them by believing them and giving them our attention and energy. I have a client who used to fall into debilitating anxiety every time an illness-related post showed up on her social media feed. As soon as she deleted the platform from her phone, her anxiety dropped significantly. When we feed fearful thoughts our vital energy, we're drawn back to them again and again in an unconscious attempt to regain our energy. Once we mindlessly lose energy, we feel compelled to go and "find it," however, this is a trap because most of the distractions that we pour our energy into are either unable or unwilling to reciprocate.

The process of reclaiming our energy involves becoming still rather than going back to the original source to try to find it. This is counter-intuitive but stillness draws our energy back to us like a magnet. The moment you realize that you've slipped into reverse flow by over-thinking, endless scrolling, or trying to convince someone of something, STOP. Initially you may feel an inner pull to keep seeking what you've lost, but soon you'll feel your yourself filling up from the inside as your natural energy returns. This is your flow. The process is always the same—we simply drop into stillness and allow our physical, emotional, and mental levels of self to come into alignment so that our energy can once again begin to flow.

The word dis-traction reveals what happens when we latch our attention onto something non-reciprocal and incapable of giving back—we lose traction and any momentum we've generated. Feeding our energy to a non-reciprocal source (including a thought virus, social media feed, or energy vampire) diverts precious energy out of our flow channel and feeds it to another source.

This kind of distraction isn't the same as being interrupted by a child or a well-meaning colleague. Living distraction-free is unrealistic, but identifying the non-reciprocal systems that we feed empowers us to reclaim our energy and seal the holes in our flow channel. Becoming the master of our attention rather than its servant is how we disrupt this first stage of reverse flow and preserve the quantity and quality of our energy.

Treasure Hunt

Think of reclaiming your energy as a treasure hunt. In a notebook or journal, write down every person, place, or activity that you've given your energy to without receiving anything meaningful in return. Hint: Anything or anyone that you're compulsively drawn to may hold a piece of your energy. Do this exercise without too much thought, but if emotion arises in response to something you write down, put a star next to it so that you know which items hold the most charge. The key is to not get stuck on any one item but to keep writing until nothing else comes to mind.

Once your list is complete, take some time to revisit each item on your list with the intention of reclaiming your energy. Once you go through each item on your list and visualize your energy coming back to you, choose what kind of relationship you'd like to have with that person, place, or activity in the future.

Leveling Up

Like the roots of a tree, presence is foundational for flow. Once we receive energy in presence, we're in a position to manage it in a way that supports our flow. We've talked about the benefits of presence and how we lose energy through chronic stress, toxic environments, and distraction. We talked about how to practice presence and the importance of energy awareness. Now let's look at the gifts of presence.

The gifts of Presence are *connection* and *clarity*. Presence connects us to ourselves and to one another and initiates the flow of energy and information. In presence, we're nourished and renewed, as are our relationships. The energy and information received brings clarity and insights that we don't get when we're distracted. Energy naturally seeks flow, and practicing presence brings whatever's not flowing into our awareness. Recognizing where you're a little stuck is good and a sign that your aligned and in your flow.

While it might be tempting to make fast changes in response to increased clarity, it's important not to get ahead of ourselves, as clarity is only the first step in the process of growth and transformation. Of course, make any changes that feel right, but when it comes to big changes, it's best to wait until the energy has had a chance to accumulate and you are "moved" from the inside out. As you continue to practice presence and bring more energy into your flow channel, you'll receive more and more clarity about what is and isn't flowing in your life. When we can witness what's not flowing without acting impulsively or distracting ourselves from what's real, we are carried to the next level where conviction accompanies clarity. The gifts of presence are endless once we align with the stream of natural abundance flowing through us. Just as a tree never abandons its roots, we remain present and connected through each stage of the flow process. The second step of the Blueprint is Energy Integrity, which is where we integrate and manage the energy we've received.

"Take responsibility for the energy you bring."

Jill Bolte Taylor

5

Energy Integrity—Your Trunk

IN THE BOOK *The Four Agreements*, Don Miguel Ruiz taught us to be impeccable with our word. The second step of the *Energy Wellness Blueprint* challenges us to be impeccable with our energy. Represented by the trunk of your tree, Energy Integrity involves taking full responsibility for your personal energy and managing it in a way that promotes inner flow. This involves protecting your energy from unnecessary drains and taking the time to process the information received in presence. Processing our experiences allows us move forward with integrity (integration + right action), which is how we stay open and flowing on the inside.

Key Energy Integrity practices include *energy management* and cultivating healthy *emotional flow*.

Energy Management

Energy is life. It fuels our wellbeing, growth, and purpose. Adopting an energy responsibility mindset puts us in charge of our personal energy and prevents us from being pushed and pulled by external forces. When we're responsible for a small child, we keep our eyes on them to protect them from harm. Likewise, protecting our energy is our sole responsibility and only something that we can do. Many of us carry beliefs about how we "should" spend our time and energy. Some of these beliefs include being there for others no matter what or "living like there's no tomorrow" at the expense of our wellbeing and flow. Others have "caught" the societal belief that chronic stress is normal and even a hallmark of success. Cultivating an energy responsibility mindset allows us to transcend some of these societal beliefs in favor of aligning with our natural flow design.

Sometimes we fear that prioritizing our energy will cause people to think that we're selfish or that life will become boring, however, this couldn't be further from the truth. Prioritizing our energy makes us more, not less, present to others, and living in our own flow is far from boring; it's an exhilarating ride that never ends. Over time, our flow channel gets bigger and bigger as does our capacity to channel energy into the world. This means more creativity, joy, love and fulfillment. Flow is the ultimate high—there is absolutely nothing that compares. As with everything, the idea of protecting our energy and giving from a place of fullness is not absolute. We all have obligations and there are times when we need to be there for others even when we're exhausted. But for every genuine responsibility we have, there are a hundred ways that we lose energy unnecessarily.

Managing Energy Instead of Stress

What if we started managing our energy instead of our stress? Protecting your energy from unnecessary drains is the simplest form of stress prevention—it increases resilience and ensures that you don't lose energy before you've fully digested it. Just as food digests without our conscious effort, energy digestion occurs naturally, but what happens, for example, if the food you've eaten isn't able to reach your stomach? It would remain undigested and you wouldn't receive the nutrients (information) or vitality (inspiration) it contains. For many of us, this is what's happening to our personal energy. Not only is it common to lose energy before we've had a chance to fully digest it, but we're often so busy that we don't adequately process the energy and information that we *do* receive.

All flow systems have the current that flows and the landscape through which it flows. This is as true for energy flow as it is for river flow, and managing our energy creates a boundaried channel through which energy can flow. The term "boundary" has many connotations and can sound negative, but when it comes to energy wellness, we need boundaries to protect the current moving through us. When we say no to what drains us, our energy has a chance to fill us up and guide us to a resounding YES! This is not about avoiding the hard things in life, it's about protecting our current from the people and things that don't support our flow.

Vibe Tracker

Just as recording what we eat increases awareness and helps us make better food choices, recording how different activities affect our "vibe" creates a feedback loop that inspires positive change. Humans have the capacity for tremendous creativity and productivity when we take full responsibility for our personal energy and seal the holes in our flow channel. Each time we pivot from something draining to something nourishing, we change our inner landscape to accommodate more flow.

I recommend tracking your energy for seven days to see how different activities and interactions affect your vibe. This will provide a clear picture of what drains you and what enlivens you. Everything has an energy signature or vibrational quality, and the more resonant it is (the more we resonate or relate to it), the better it feels. Walking your dog might feel like a "high vibe" activity, while a sensational news story might be experienced as "low vibe." We experience different vibrations *in our body*, so try not to overthink it. Instead, use embodied awareness to see how your energy responds to various people, places, and things. Because this is highly subjective (what one person finds draining, another could find energizing), it is *your vibe* that you're tracking rather than the vibe of the thing itself. In general, things that feel "high vibe" will add to the quality and quantity of your energy and will feel uplifting, inspiring, or energizing, while things that feel "low vibe" will decrease the quality and quantity of your energy and feel draining, negative, or toxic.

Use your energy as a barometer and release any preconceived notions about what is and isn't high vibe. You might spend an hour talking to a friend who's struggling and log it as "high vibe," not because the topic was positive but because the interaction was authentic and heart based. This is an opportunity to become more attuned to your energy and how it responds to different activities. Remember that our energy communicates with us on four distinct wavelengths: physical, emotional, mental, and spiritual/energetic. Be as specific as you can when describing the various sensations, moods, thoughts, and vibe associated with each activity. Words like queasy, exhilarating, or heavy are more descriptive than just simply saying "high vibe" or "low vibe."

Identifying Blind Spots

There's a subtle layer of energy that lies just below the surface of our awareness. This subterranean part of our landscape acts as a safe haven for our blind spots. It's common to unknowingly lose energy through words that we speak, thoughts that we think, and the ways that we communicate with others. Without examining ourselves through a microscope, which often does more harm than good, we can become aware of when we compromise our own energy simply by noticing how we feel after engaging in certain behaviors.

In general, the clearer you become the more finely attuned you are to the energy within and around you. And when an emotion or experience is not digesting well, you'll feel this in your body as something unfinished and in need of your attention. The tendency is to want to blame someone or something and spend a lot of time worrying or talking about it, but more often than not, when we're unable to digest a situation, it's because we haven't taken responsibility for our part of a dynamic. Perhaps we spoke about someone in a way that was exaggerative and unkind. Maybe we talked over someone in a conflict rather than listening and trying to understand them. Maybe we didn't say something when we should have. You get the idea: at this subtle level, part of the equation is us. Practicing energy integrity allows us to identify our part of a dynamic so that we can clean it up as soon as possible. Sometimes we feel the need to make amends to someone, and other times it's enough to reflect within and simply identify our part. Energy blocks serve an important purpose—they move our blind spots out of the shadows so that our energy can reach these areas and refine the patterns blocking our flow. We know our energy is blocked when our mind starts spinning and our emotions become heavy or stuck. One thing's for sure, *blaming and projecting is the opposite of integrating.* It's amazing how easy it is to release grievances when we identify our part of a challenging dynamic—even if it's the tiniest part. Taking responsibility for our contribution is how we untangle from situations that would otherwise steal our peace. With more space on the inside, we get to travel lighter and experience more flow.

Karma

What exactly is karma? In my experience, karma is a combination of unprocessed energy and unintegrated opportunities for growth. The boomerang effect of karma is our own energy drawing us back to similar situations to get resolution. This "cycle" repeats over and over, not because there's a vengeful God out there wanting to torture us but because we unconsciously resonate with situations that bring us opportunities for integration. This perspective on karma highlights why it's important to take responsibility for the quality of our thoughts, words, and interactions—keeping our part of a situation clean means that we don't have to clean it up later. We all make an energetic mess from time to time and infuse our words with bad mojo but the sooner we recognize it and make it right, the better. Our "why" is not to be a good person—although that's wonderful—rather, it's to become a *clear* channel through which energy can flow.

Emotional Flow

Emotion is energy in motion. Because emotions can be hard to digest, it's easy to gloss over them and pretend that they're not even there. These pockets of unprocessed emotion become like boulders in our river that slow and sometimes even block our flow. Acknowledging and processing our emotions helps us digest and interpret the energy that's trying to move through us.

We create the conditions for emotional flow by finding the balance between over-containment and over-expression—having a flow channel that's neither too tight nor too loose. Most people fall to one side or the other, leaning more toward over-containing or over-expressing their emotions. The key is to contain our emotions long enough to process them but not so long that we suppress or avoid them. Again, think of food—it needs to be in our stomach long enough to digest but not so long that it rots there. When we over-contain our emotions, the energy backs up and we run the risk of exploding at inopportune times. We also become energetically congested, which can manifest as depression, anxiety, and overwhelm.

In the case of over-expression, emotional energy is released before it's been fully digested. This impacts our ability to process intense emotions and lowers our natural resilience. Intense emotions are simply a high velocity of energy moving through us and when we release emotional energy prematurely, we lose the opportunity to gain real insight on a situation. Losing emotional energy also makes us more vulnerable to power struggles because of the unconscious drive to get our energy back once we've lost it. There's only one way to regain energy that's lost in a power struggle: let go of the need to be right and reconnect with the stream of energy moving through you, which is your real lifeline and source of stability.

Just as we are a container through which energy flows, our relationships become their own container with their own flow landscape. When we explode or "dump" emotions on another person, this not only weakens our own container but can also damage the relational container. Likewise, habitually withholding feelings robs the relationship of fresh energy and the connection needed to sustain the bond. Finding ways to process and communicate our feelings is key for both the over-container and the over-expresser, as it prevents energy from building up within us and between us and strengthens our relational container.

Close relationships mirror our inner flow landscape and offer the opportunity to fast-track our return to flow. But because relational patterns are often so charged, it can be hard to identify where blind spots are running the show. Temporarily holding onto your energy rather than impulsively reacting is like getting a body scan with contrast dye—the energy within lights up the areas where flow is obstructed. The willingness to see and feel what was previously hidden clears the lens of perception and allows us to see more clearly.

Finding the balance between emotional containment and expression not only changes our own inner landscape but also changes the landscape of our relationships. This is ultimately positive but can feel unfamiliar or uncomfortable for a time. It's like having two puzzle pieces that fit together perfectly but then changing the shape of your piece so that it's more balanced. The idea is not to disrupt the harmony of a relationship but to increase personal and relational flow. It's best to allow the relationship time to adjust, as when one person becomes more emotionally integrated, it invites the other to do the same. The process of increasing relational wellness and flow is the exact same as increasing personal wellness and flow. It only takes one person to practice presence and energy integrity, and then transformation follows. One way or another, things change and this is good. Life is not designed to stay static, it is designed to flow, and as a result, landscapes change, adapt, and at times, veer off in different directions.

Thinking Pulls Us Out of Feeling

We all know the feeling of being "stuck" in frustration or "wallowing" in sadness. While it can and often does take time for intense emotional energy to become refined enough to move through us, the way we think about our feelings will either support or hinder this process.

In short, *thinking pulls us out of feeling* and obstructs emotional flow. While it's good to identify what you're feeling and what triggered a certain reaction, obsessing or ruminating about what happened is rarely helpful. Once you've taken some time to reflect on how you're feeling, it's best to drop your awareness into your body and just be with the emotion. Depending on the intensity, it can be helpful to engage in some movement or exercise, as this moves the energy and often brings clarity and relief. Sometimes, as with a big loss or major life change, we enter a season of emotion that we just need to move through. These transformational times are part of life's natural flow and it's especially important to be compassionate with ourselves during these extended periods of emotional intensity.

Almost everyone I talk to describes themselves as an "over-thinker" and experiences pressure or energy congestion in their head. Making it a habit to keep our energy evenly distributed throughout our body prevents us from "getting stuck" in our head. When we're balanced and aligned, our thinking mind works in harmony with the other levels of self (physical, emotional, spiritual) to promote wellbeing and flow. Overthinking is an obstacle to flow—reclaiming our energy from repetitive thought loops is totally doable and gets easier as we become the master of our attention instead of its servant. Practicing presence in whatever way works for you (meditation, mindful breathing, etc.) accelerates the dissolution of energy-draining mental patterns and promotes neuroplasticity.

Emotional Whirlpools

Emotional whirlpools are energy consuming patterns that are fueled by our thinking. It's helpful to identify the whirlpools that exist in our mind/body flow channel. We often refer to these patterns as "triggers," which is appropriate because they usually form in response to a specific event or time in our life. However, on top of the original wound, which is really a piece of unintegrated energy, are layers of mental and emotional congestion that build up each time the pattern is activated and fed mental energy.

Healing trauma is beyond the scope of this book, but it is helpful to become aware of the triggers that pull us out of our flow and the stories that keep them locked in place. Once we identify the stories that perpetuate the patterns, we can change the narrative to more accurately reflect present moment circumstances and take some of the charge out of them. Becoming aware of our emotional whirlpools is how we become *bigger* than our patterns and less likely to be taken over by them. Think of yourself as a river and the whirlpools as part of your river. Rather than trying to get rid of them, our emphasis should be staying connected to our body and breath and not feeding them mental energy when they're activated. Like water flowing through a canyon, our abundant inner flow refines our triggers over time.

Just as a nourishing environment is essential for growing strong roots, being around people who respect our feelings and boundaries is essential for maintaining our flow. As I shared in the chapter on Presence, we naturally shut down when we perceive an environment to be unsafe. While "shutting down" and becoming more guarded can be an effective way to protect our energy, being in a hostile environment long-term is not good for us and impacts our ability process emotions.

We can survive, and potentially even thrive for a time, however, it's best to surround ourselves with people who allow us to be a little messy and imperfect as we find our way and grow into our full expression.

Clarity and Conviction

While Presence brings clarity, Energy Integrity brings conviction. The more we integrate and lean into our inner experience without reacting, avoiding, or suppressing, the more conviction accumulates in our body and the more we *know* what's right for us. Energy digestion activates our "gut instincts." Often, the knowing is immediate, but sometimes, even when we've received waves of clarity, we're still not sure what to do. When we're willing to continuously feel the truth of a situation without jumping out of our flow stream, the polarization of "should I or shouldn't I" alchemizes over time and explodes into conviction. Sometimes, as with major life decisions, we may need to wait until the energy within reaches our heart and transforms into the courage of a lion (this happens at the next stage). One thing's for sure, when we remain present and aligned with our flow, the energy will move us to act when the time is right.

Reverse Flow Pathway

In the section on Presence, we identified *distraction* as the first step on the reverse flow pathway. The second stage of reverse flow is *avoidance*—we know what we need to do to get back into alignment but consciously or unconsciously avoid taking the steps to do so. Avoidance leads to energy fragmentation instead of energy integration and flow. Instead of integrating the energy we receive, the current becomes fragmented through suppression (emotional avoidance), chronic stress (energy drains), or over-thinking (spinning energy). Fragmented energy can't flow. This leads to feeling empty, which perpetuates the chase and keeps us stuck in the reverse flow loop. The good news is that we can move back into alignment any time by becoming present and reconnecting to the energy within.

Leveling Up

Energy Integrity creates the conditions for inner flow by cultivating an open and boundaried channel through which energy can flow. In addition to increasing emotional flow, processing the energy we receive brings insights and information that we may have otherwise missed. Leaning into our feelings and inner knowing fast tracks energy wellness and puts us squarely on our purpose path.

We explored the benefits of managing our energy instead of our stress and the challenges to Energy Integrity including over-thinking and emotional whirlpools. We looked at how intense emotions reveal blind spots and how to transform our triggers by becoming bigger than our patterns and allowing our energy to buff them out.

The gifts of Energy Integrity are *resilience* and *well-being*. More energy means more resilience and the ability to respond to life's challenges with agility, and processing life as it occurs keeps us flowing on the inside and prevents emotions from building up and weighing us down. This translates to wellbeing—the feeling of inner peace that accompanies healthy emotional flow. This brings us to the third step, which is Transformation and the natural growth that occurs when we apply our energy according to our inner knowing.

Transformation isn't something we control, it's something we allow.

6

Transformation— Your Branches

THE THIRD STEP of the *Energy Wellness Blueprint* is Transformation, which corresponds to the branches of your tree and the organic growth that takes place when we act in alignment with our inner knowing. While change is inevitable, transformation depends on our ability to manage our energy in a way that supports our growth. Solid roots (Presence) and a strong trunk (Energy Integrity) are required to grow new branches. Transformation isn't something we control, it's something we *allow*. Once we act in alignment with our inner knowing, it's time to release our attachment to the outcome and let the energy work its magic and carve out new pathways in our life. Transformation keeps us fresh and expands our capacity for flow. The practices that support this stage of flow are *right action* and *releasing attachment*.

Flow Power

Transforming energy into action is a powerful act of will, and once our energy gets to this level, we become power generators. The inside-out flow of energy produces a different type of power than we're used to seeing. Flow power is the inside-out momentum that's generated when we live in alignment with our natural design. This type of power nourishes, rather than depletes, the broader flow systems that we're a part of. An example of this is a leader who practices transparency and follows through on their word. Things may not always go as planned, but because the leader is trusted, everyone does their best and there's abundant energy flow within the team in the form of communication, laughter, innovation, and productivity.

Transformation—Your Branches

Transformation is an extension of Energy Integrity. Because we're integrating our energy, we naturally know what to do next—*we know what needs to be done to preserve the river of peace that arises when we refuse to avoid, suppress, or compartmentalize our energy.* There's an integrity crisis in the world today, and some people are clearly operating from a different handbook than that of nature. This book is for those who wish to experience abundant inner peace and a more harmonious world—those who are powered by love energy as I described earlier. Those who choose to withhold information rather than be transparent, manipulate instead of collaborate, and control outcomes rather than allow transformation are not operating in alignment with nature and will not be able to hold their power in the long term. This old version of power is unsustainable and ultimately destructive because in the absence of inner flow, one can never get enough.

Many of us live and work in environments that continue to operate on old power paradigms, however, the more aligned and integrated we become, the more painful it is to remain in these environments. The lack of environmental flow becomes palpable and we're no longer able to tolerate the inner dissonance it creates. This third stage of flow is where we really start to untangle from these systems and all that's siphoning our energy. This can take time, but staying present and acting with integrity is how we slowly—or sometimes quickly—untangle from the people and systems operating on old power.

Taking Right Action

Acting on our inner knowing is as much about timing as it is about the action itself. Earlier we explored time as a river of energy. As this river moves through us, we first get clarity, then conviction, and finally courage. Courage comes when the energy of conviction accumulates within and rises to the level of our heart. The heart integrates thinking (the mind) and knowing (the body) and delivers us to a crossroads where we must make a choice: either act in alignment with our knowing and preserve our flow or split the river within and delay right action. I refer to this choice point as *riding the wave*. If we miss the wave, we'll have to wait for another one to come around. If we miss the wave too many times, a tidal wave comes and takes care of it for us—like it or not, we're carried forward. This "gift from the universe" occurs when the pent-up energy is no longer able to contain itself. No one can escape the incoming flow that periodically changes the landscape of our life—nor should we try. When we try to outrun or delay the inevitable, nature forces our hand and we experience *forced transformation* instead of the natural change that occurs when we move in alignment with our inner knowing.

Transformation often brings up fear because it's impossible to predict how the landscape of our life will change in response to right action. In this sense, it's understandable and natural to delay big decisions until we're ready, but if we delay for too long, we squeeze grace out of the process. Grace is the flow of energy that carries us on its current. This inner momentum doesn't get rid of the fear, it simply supports us on the inside and paves the way for a gentler transition.

Flow Is Not Linear

Although I'm presenting flow as a step by step process, it's not a linear journey. Some decisions are so big that we need to go back to the beginning a hundred times. We may alternate between confusion and clarity for what feels like forever, but in the midst of confusion we can return to presence again and again. We take baby steps, make mistakes, and f… it up over and over. This is what flow really looks like. We weave in and out of alignment and the opportunity for refinement lies in our ability to *honor the process and trust ourselves*. The more time we spend in our own flow, the easier it is to return when we veer off course. Alignment becomes a habit that's reinforced every time we course correct. We're incentivized to course correct because of how good alignment feels. I'd rather have inner peace than inner chaos any day, even though the peace path requires far more courage and contains many more unknowns.

Fast Flow and Slow Flow

We can think of organic growth and transformation in terms of *fast flow* and *slow flow*. Fast flow is more about the small choices we make each day to honor our energy. We weave in and out of social interactions using vibes as our radar, we get water when we're thirsty, and go for walks when we need to move or decompress. We follow the inner current moment by moment, and when we notice that we've drifted, we quickly move back into alignment: we put the phone down, stop fighting with our partner, or push away the dessert. Most of these fast decisions happen at the first two stages of flow as we practice presence and intentionally manage our energy throughout the day.

Slow flow is the longer process of change and growth that shapes our life over time. Both fast flow and slow flow have the power to transform us, as we all know the power of our everyday choices to change us over time. Slow flow refers to the longer transformational cycles that we all go through—the long journey toward mastery, the sad ending of a relationship, or the inevitable loss of a parent. These changes are a natural part of life's flow. Branches grow and they also fall away. Sustainable energy wellness depends on our ability to periodically transform, otherwise, we get stuck and stagnate. When energy can't properly flow, whether it's emotional energy, physical energy, or relational energy, it turns against us and wreaks havoc on our mind, body, and life.

Releasing Attachment

Transformation requires that we release attachment to a specific outcome, as releasing control is the only way to remain in integrity and stay in our flow. This doesn't mean that we don't have strong preferences and work hard toward a desired outcome, it just means that we aren't willing to sacrifice the integrity of the process to achieve a specific outcome. In flow, the end never justifies the means. The energy shapes the final outcome. And because we're nested within larger flow systems (relationships, family, organizations), our increased flow impacts the entire system. If a relationship or team isn't flowing, aligning with your own flow invites others to do the same. Part of releasing attachment is not worrying too much about what others will think, feel, or do in response to your aligned choices. Seeing it for what it is—an invitation—prevents us from second guessing ourselves or worrying about how others will respond.

Staying Aligned in the Midst of Struggle

What does it look like to stay aligned when something in your life isn't flowing? Think of the last time you we're in a stagnant relationship—going through the motions but not feeling any flow. Alignment might look like practicing radical presence and noticing what happens the next time you genuinely try to connect, but it goes nowhere. A reverse flow response to the pain of not being received would be to start a fight, overconsume, or zone out on your phone, but because you're committed to staying aligned and in your flow, you walk away—perhaps into a room where you have some privacy—and *feel* the pain of disconnection. You may shed a few tears, you may experience a wave of anger, or you may feel confused and wonder what the hell to do. If you're not sure what to do, just keep observing and feeling (Presence and Energy Integrity) without reacting and falling into reverse flow behaviors that cause you to lose energy. Over time, the energy builds; first you receive clarity about what's happening, then conviction: *This is NOT working for me.* Eventually the rising energy reaches your heart. The moment it does, *you know what to do and have the courage to do it.* Perhaps you decide to tell the person that you feel disconnected and that you long for a deeper relationship. While this may seem easy enough, this level of honesty is highly vulnerable, which is why it requires courage. You then observe the response (Presence) and feel the feelings (Energy Integrity), refusing to numb or distract yourself from what's happening. You get the idea. Eventually the relationship transforms in response to you practicing integrity (integration + right action); either things change or you reach a crossroads in which you must make a choice to preserve the peace within.

When we get to this point in the process, we've grown and are no longer the same person we were. The

Transformation — Your Branches

alternative is to accept the status quo and continue the relationship with form but no substance or leave and find another relationship without having grown. There is only one organic path to growth, and when we honor this process, we not only transform into a more evolved version of ourselves, but we also experience increased energy wellness due to our high levels of inner clarity and flow. When we side-step the process and either stagnate or make only superficial changes, we do so with a suitcase of unintegrated energy. This is the real meaning of emotional baggage. It's not precious children, a mortgage, or quirky in-laws, it's unfinished business that will one day have to be reconciled.

This same process applies to every situation in which you feel stuck—a job that's become unfulfilling, a habit that you can't shake, or any other situation that has you feeling down. If we can stay in the process and not get ahead of ourselves, the energy transforms us from the inside out. No program or guru can do this for you, which is why living in alignment with your own flow is the ultimate hero's journey—you are the hero in your journey.

Reverse Flow Pathway

We explored the first two stages of flow and their corresponding reverse flow pathways: *Presence* versus *distraction* and *Energy Integrity* versus *avoidance*. This brings us to the third stage of reverse flow which is *compensation*. Because our energy has been diverted through distraction, fragmented through avoidance, and buried in suppression, the only option is to compensate for a lack of inner flow. At this stage, reverse-flow behaviors become more entrenched and habitual. Everyone has their preferred compensation strategies and ways of coping with the weight of unexpressed energy, but ultimately, they don't work. They may offer temporary relief but only at the cost of continued suppression and inner angst. Because we're designed for flow, the energy within will not stop pressing on us until we get back into alignment and integrate what we're carrying. Until then, we'll be driven to compensate with behaviors that numb and distract us from feeling what's real.

Transformation—Your Branches

This stage of reverse flow culminates in a stress spiral—a race to outrun oneself. No one is immune and we all end up compensating for a lack of flow at some point, often just prior to making a major change. And because change is scary, the impulse to keep going in the wrong direction is strong—we instinctively know that if we stop running, the energy will surface and we'll have to feel what we've previously avoided. This is nothing to worry about, however, because the energy doesn't come all at once. It comes in waves and we can handle it.

We all know the feeling of returning to our flow after being out of alignment for some time. Depending on the compensation strategy, this might look like giving up booze, facing our debt, or getting off technology. While we can delay the inevitable, we can't outrun ourselves forever. Just like the parable of the prodigal son, the energy within welcomes us with open arms no matter how long we've been away. We simply connect in presence and receive what's there. It doesn't matter how messy things appear, only that we're moving in the right direction—inside-out rather than outside-in.

Often the stakes aren't so high. Perhaps we've stopped exercising or neglected to express our feelings to someone close to us. Maybe we've allowed something to go on for too long, like consuming too many creature comforts that we'd rather not give up. It's important not to beat ourselves up if we've been out of flow for a minute, as this will only keep us stuck. When we stay present and open rather than guilting ourselves, our natural energy returns and supports us to make a different choice.

Reverse Flow Checklist

Compensation strategies come in many shapes and sizes, often disguising themselves as habits. These habits of mind and body can become so engrained that we often don't realize that they're compensating for a lack of flow in some other area of our life. Below is a list of reverse flow behaviors commonly used to compensate for a lack of flow. These behaviors aren't inherently "bad" but can be relied upon to generate stress energy and cheap dopamine or avoid suppressed emotions. One might use a mental habit such as worrying to compensate for a lack of emotional flow or a physical habit like substance use to compensate for a lack of spiritual or relational flow.

Transformation—Your Branches

_____ Mindless eating

_____ Substance use

_____ Over-busyness

_____ Excessive exercise

_____ Sleeping

_____ Shopping

_____ Gaming

_____ Social Media/dating apps

_____ Gambling/sex addiction

_____ Procrastination

_____ Control

_____ Binge watching videos/shows

_____ Worrying/catastrophic thinking

_____ Stressing out over little things

_____ Rushing

_____ Complaining/gossiping

_____ Rescuing/over-giving

_____ Chronic conflict or avoidance

_____ Emotional exploding or imploding

_____ Victimization/poor me thinking

_____ Perfectionism

_____ Over-thinking

Untangling from Compensation Strategies

We untangle from reverse flow and our habitual compensation strategies in the exact same way that we untangle from everything else that drains and distracts us from our purpose path—we draw our energy back to us by practicing presence. We may not be able to stop the compensation strategy immediately, but we remain present and embodied whenever we engage with it. We notice what happens with our energy and how we feel before, during, and after engaging in the behavior. We process and integrate the impact that the behavior has on our wellbeing and relationships, and when we're ready, we make a different choice. Maybe it's a baby step like skipping a day or even delaying the activity until after exercise. Over time, our non-judgement and flowing energy loosens the grip that the habit has on us and our inner landscape begins to open up. Soon, we get our energy back and our power quickly follows. We are once again in the driver's seat where we can steer our energy and move forward instead of in circles.

Leveling Up

In this third step, we explored the connection between integrity and growth. Allowing our lives to transform in response to right action requires tremendous courage, but it's the only path to organic growth—a tree cannot jump ahead and expediently produce fruit; it stays in its process, and as a result, comes to fruition. Staying in our process and not jumping ahead bridges the gap between wellbeing (inner flow) and purpose (outer flow)—we keep doing the next right thing and continuously move toward mastery in every area of our life.

We emphasized the importance of releasing attachment to the outcome and the grace of flow that follows. We also identified the third step of reverse flow, which is *compensation* and the impulse to chase energy when we're not flowing. The gifts of Transformation are *growth and expansion*. In short, we've increased our *capacity for flow*. We've strengthened our branches, released that which no longer flows, and moved toward mastery in key areas of our life. This brings us to the final step of the Blueprint, which is Flow itself.

Flow is the seamless expression of your energy into the world.

7

Flow—Your Fruit

THE FIRST THREE STEPS of the *Energy Wellness Blueprint*—Presence, Energy Integrity, and Transformation—culminate in Flow, which is the seamless expression of your energy into the world. Flow corresponds to the fruit of your tree and the gifts you share with the world. Living in alignment with our own flow is how we grow into fruition. The first three steps fill us with energy and prepare us to create, connect, and express ourselves in new ways. That said, *our energy flows even when we're still,* which is why living from a place of fullness makes our presence even more of a gift. You can be sitting quietly in an airport and a stranger walking by will sense your high vibrational energy. When aligned and in our flow, we become a source of nourishment and positivity for those around us. We continuously expand our flow by taking *mindful risks* and practicing a *growth mindset*.

Sharing Your Energy with the World

When it comes to energy wellness, *flow* is the goal, as it's the only thing that fuels us with the high-quality energy that we crave. Flow is nature's pathway for a reason—it both nourishes and evolves us. Although flow is a seamless process, we can view it as both inner and outer: the first three steps promote inner flow, while this last step promotes outer flow as our energy extends into the world as productivity, passion, creativity, love, and high vibes. Energy wellness depends on this last step as *we are not full until we give what we have away.*

We long for meaningful contribution—simply having energy is not enough. It's the movement of energy that we crave and the act of giving that drives us. When we sit on the current moving through us rather than express it, our energy starts spinning instead of flowing.

We call this stress, and in its more extreme form, anxiety. In this sense, expressing our unique energy, voice, and contributions is a form of self-care. To illustrate this truth, just consider how painful it is to not express yourself. *Not expressing ourselves goes against our natural design and ultimately destroys us.*

The second law of thermodynamics states that a system in isolation gradually moves toward chaos—this is what happens when we feel disconnected from the world around us. Instead of our energy flowing, it turns against us and wreaks havoc with our mind and emotions. Like nature, each of us has a part to play in the greater flow of life. When we aren't able to add our voice and unique contribution to the world around us, we *feel* isolated. You are an essential part of the whole and being with those who value your contribution is a gift indeed. Sometimes, we're not sure exactly what our part is but if we can stay aligned with our own flow, we'll eventually find ourselves in a place where what we have to give is exactly what's needed.

Flow is Disruptive

Just as it's never been more important to practice presence, it's never been more important to add our energy to the world. Sometimes this involves ruffling some feathers, rocking a boat, or whatever other euphemism comes to mind. When we move through life aligned, integrated, and flowing, our very presence shines a light on what isn't flowing. Like a river that clears out anything in its path, we naturally disrupt anything that's stagnant. As uncomfortable as this can be at times, it's important to acknowledge this unspoken truth—flowing energy naturally seeps into the places that are hidden and stuck. This applies to both our inner and outer world.

Surface harmony is a mask for blocked flow and disrupting this façade is okay, and in many ways, out of our control. It's the energy that disrupts, not our ego. We're not *trying* to get the energy moving, it just happens. When aligned, we can easily feel what is and isn't flowing, whether it be an individual, a relationship, or a team, but if we forsake our own alignment to preserve surface harmony, we ourselves become stuck.

This looks like pretending to be happy when we're not, agreeing when we don't, and passively observing while others control the flow of interpersonal energy and information. Sometimes people try block other's flow on purpose, but eventually the dam will break—as energy cannot be held back forever. If one is intent on damming another's flow for the sake of accumulating more of what they seek, our flowing energy will be viewed as negative. This is out of our control. All we can do is show up to our lives aligned and in integrity—the stuck situations we encounter will either transform or we will move on.

It's essential for our long-term mental health to live and work in environments that are able to *receive* us. Of course, we need to be mindful not to put ourselves in harm's way but putting a lid on our outer flow after cultivating healthy inner flow is even more painful than being out of alignment all together. At this stage, our energy is ready is waiting to emerge like a blossoming flower. It's critical that we give what we have away as giving completes the cycle and brings fresh energy into our mind/body flow channel so that we can do it all over again.

Taking Mindful Risks

Just as your younger self liked to push the limits and take some risks (hopefully not too many!), living in flow requires that we expand beyond our comfort zone. Taking mindful risks pushes us to the edge of our growth and carves out new flow pathways. This is why time in the zone is associated with mastery—moving toward mastery in any area of life refines the pathways through which energy flows (neuropathways, emotional pathways, creative pathways, and relational pathways). The more refined the pathway, the more time in flow.

Pushing the boundaries of our expression is how we collectively evolve, as it only takes one person to show us a whole new way of being. Carving out new pathways takes time and requires faith in your vision. That's all we receive at first—a vision of how things could be or how *we* could be. We start from there—like cross country skiing after a fresh snow. We carve out the pathway inch by inch. First our inner world changes—our neuro network expands, we develop new skills, and our passion grows as our energy rises. As we show up day after day, our environment changes to accommodate the increased output—the world receives us. We are powered by the same energy that created the universe—our job is to harness this power and apply it toward that which lights us up. Consistency is key but so is balance. Those who bring new ways of being to the world know when to push forward and when to pause or pivot. The question becomes, *how do we move forward without getting overwhelmed?*

Balancing Challenge and Skill

Mihaly Csikszentmihalyi, author of the groundbreaking book *Flow: The Psychology of Optimal Experience*, emphasized the importance of balancing challenge and skill, saying, "Enjoyment appears at the boundary between boredom and anxiety when the challenges are just balanced with the person's capacity to act."[2] Studying creatives, Csikszentmihalyi found that if the challenge of a situation is too high, we become anxious,

---

[2] Csikszentmihalyi, Mihaly. *Flow: The Psychology of Optimal Experience.* New York: Harper & Row, 1990), 52.

but if our skill far outsizes the challenge, we become bored. Therefore, while it's important not to push ourselves too far, once we've reached a certain level of mastery in any area of life, we need to keep going, lest we become bored and lose the excitement that flow brings.

This same principle applies to energy wellness—when life becomes too challenging, our flow channel constricts and our mind starts racing. This tells our body that something's wrong and that it needs to prepare to fight, flee, or freeze. Before we know it, we're swimming in stress energy. Returning to a state of inner and outer flow involves relaxing our mind/body flow channel and expanding our awareness so that we're not funneling all our energy into mental activity. Both anxiety and boredom compromise our ability to flow. While anxiety constricts our flow channel, boredom is like a river with no borders, leaving us dry and looking for energy in all the wrong places. This low-flow state indicates our flow channel is too loose and that we need to direct our energy toward something meaningful. Placing our attention on a new goal or challenge reignites our flow and tightens an overly-relaxed and lethargic flow channel. Your energy will tell you if your flow channel too tight (anxious) or too loose (bored)—boredom is your energy asking for greater expression, while feeling anxious or overwhelmed is a cue to take your foot off the gas and slow down for a minute.

Sometimes "unlearning" a routine is needed to increase our flow. Flow pathways become increasingly engrained over time, and because energy flows down the path of least resistance, our habits can become big energy consumers. In this case, we can expand our capacity for flow by *not* doing what we've always done. Perhaps we make the choice to stop checking our phone first thing in the morning or to stop complaining about our boss. Simply doing or thinking something different pushes us out of our comfort zone and transforms redundant flow pathways.

Conditions for Personal Energy Flow

Just as focused attention, having a clear goal, and finding the balance between challenge and skill create the conditions for peak performance flow, we too *create the conditions* for personal energy flow. These conditions are the four steps outlined in this book—Presence connects us to our curiosity and reveals where the energy wants to go. Energy Integrity keeps us open and flowing on the inside while ensuring that we don't lose the vitality needed to grow into our full expression. Transformation initiated by right action moves us toward mastery and carves out new pathways for energy to flow. And Flow completes the cycle as we give what we have away and make room for more. This inside-out way of being keeps us in alignment with our natural design where wellbeing and purpose intertwine and support one another.

Passion and Purpose

Earlier we explored purpose as both micro (moment to moment) and macro (life purpose). Living in our own flow is how the seeds of our purpose grow—like an old tree, we rise in stature and power and our gifts become more and more abundant. The way we unfold is a mystery, but what we know for sure is that we're designed to grow into our full expression. To do this, we need to maintain alignment, trust the process, and allow our energy to lead. The saying, "follow your passion" is appropriate here because what is passion if not rising energy?

Following our passion pushes the boundaries of self-expression and often takes us out of our comfort zone. We make space for our passion by leaning into our curiosity. We can be curiously drawn to anything from a person we've just met to learning a new skill. Following the scent of curiosity involves noticing how your energy perks up around certain people, places, or things. You might feel warm and tingly or have a wave of quickening move through you as you pass something on the street. In these moments, there's a bounce in your energy that makes you want to lean in and learn more. Trusting even mild curiosity can take you to places you never could have imagined had you stayed in the comfort zone of your mind—just thinking about doing something is not enough, but even the smallest action can lead to new opportunities for growth and giving. It's never too late to follow a passion. At any age or stage of life, we can step into the river of our life and move with the current.

In flow, all parts of us work in synchrony—our body, emotions, thoughts, and energy move as one. We are more fluid and don't slow ourselves down with excessive analysis. When something doesn't feel right, we pivot quickly. Sometimes, we move toward something we're passionate about and quickly realize that doing the thing is harder than we thought. It's easy to get disappointed and wonder why our new pursuit isn't flowing. However, encountering resistance isn't always a sign to pivot, sometimes it just means that the pathway isn't fully formed yet. Knowing when to persist and when to pivot is an art form that requires the ability to persevere in the face of obstacles. If you walk away from something and it comes back to you again and again, that's your energy saying, "keep going… persist." Say you want to learn how to play the guitar but find that it's harder than you anticipated. If you put the guitar down and find yourself thinking about it two months later, that's an indication that the pathway is worth pursuing.

Seeds are Delicate

Using discernment about who we invite into our process of unfolding is essential to protect the delicacy of our seeds. While it's fun and sometimes helpful to share our dreams with others, it's good to wait until we've spent some time cultivating the conditions for growth before we invite someone into our garden. This involves nourishing our dream with time, attention, and energy so it can take root and become resilient to outside energies. Unfortunately, there are those who would step on your seeds of greatness and crush them into a thousand pieces. Purpose is personal, and while some will do their best to support you, others won't be able to see the potential that you carry.

In general, it's best to reserve a newly unfolding dream for those who are capable of holding the space with the reverence and respect it deserves. People respond (or unconsciously react) to our growing power and momentum in surprising ways. Sometimes, those we see as our biggest supporters let us down and unconsciously try to hold us back—perhaps because they're not growing their own seeds? Others, whom we assume don't care as much may offer sincere encouragement and watch our progress with admiration and support. Just remember, *what's yours is yours.* No one has your seeds of greatness and no one can take them from you. If the urge to do something comes back to you over and over, trust that it's yours, and no matter how others react or how many people are already doing it, your unique expression is needed and will be one of a kind.

Reflection: Assess Your Flow

This reflection is designed to help you assess your flow across five dimensions: physical, emotional, mental, spiritual and relational. When aligned, energy flows seamlessly through each level as an integrated current. The levels work in harmony to promote flow and wellbeing for the entire system. When energy isn't flowing in one area, the whole system is affected and we begin to compensate with reverse flow behaviors. In your notebook or journal, assess your current level of flow across each dimension. Note how a lack of flow in one area affects other areas of your life.

Physical Flow

We experience physical flow as vitality, alertness, and balance in our body. Physical flow is optimized when we are oxygenated, hydrated, rested, well nourished, and regulated in our nervous system (as opposed to chronically stressed or shut down). We support healthy physical flow by eating clean, hydrating, exercising, deep breathing, being in nature, and getting enough rest. Do you experience healthy physical flow most of the time? How do you compensate when you experience a lack of vitality, alertness, and balance in your body?

Emotional Flow

We experience emotional flow when we allow our feelings to move through our body in a fluid way rather than avoiding them or being taken over by them. We support emotional flow with self-awareness, self-compassion, authentic self-expression, and balancing the tendency to either over or under express. Do you experience healthy emotional flow most of the time? How do you compensate for a lack of emotional flow?

Mental Flow

We experience mental flow when we're able to balance thinking and being, and are free from excessive worry, fear, negative beliefs, and intrusive thoughts. We support mental flow with embodied awareness, mindfulness, inner stillness, and movement. Creating a balance between thinking and being supports bottom-up processing as well as more rational top-down processing. Do you experience healthy mental flow most of the time? How do you compensate for a lack of mental flow?

Relational Flow

We experience relational flow as the dynamic and reciprocal exchange of energy with those around us. Relational flow occurs when we feel supported enough to authentically express our thoughts, feelings, and needs, and allow others to do the same. We support relational flow by surrounding ourselves with people we trust, being generous with our supportive words and actions, and by facing rather than avoiding healthy conflict. Do you experience healthy relational flow with those closest to you? How do you compensate for a lack of relational flow?

Spiritual Flow

Spiritual flow is related to our purpose and a connection to something bigger than ourselves (the greater flow). We experience spiritual flow when we live on-purpose and freely share our gifts and positive presence with the world and those around us. In addition to providing a sense of purpose, spiritual flow infuses our life with meaning and creates a pathway for abundant energy flow. An absence of spiritual flow is experienced as a lack of meaning, purpose, and connection to the outer world. Do you experience spiritual or purpose-driven flow? How do you compensate when you feel a lack of spiritual flow?

In flow, everything becomes feedback.

Cultivating a Growth Mindset

Carole Dweck of Stanford University introduced us to the concept of a growth mindset.[3] People with a growth mindset believe that their abilities are dynamic and always changing while people with a fixed mindset view their abilities as, well, fixed. Those with a growth mindset embrace feedback—both good and bad—and use it to become better, while those with a fixed mindset are less receptive and therefore more static.

In flow, everything is feedback and setbacks are simply opportunities for refinement. Having a growth mindset positions us to receive feedback from within and around us so that we can quickly return to alignment when we veer off course. When we can remain aligned and flowing on the inside even when the world around us feels chaotic, we are well on our way to energy mastery. My daughter recently reminded me of the classic line in the movie Finding Nemo, "Just keep swimming…"

---

[3] Dweck, Carol. *Mindset: The New Psychology of Success.* New York: Ballantine Books, 2016.

Receiving feedback isn't always easy, and the more we put ourselves out there, the more feedback we receive. Not taking things personally is a flow superpower that allows us to maintain alignment even when the world spits us out. The reality is that not everything is for you. There are some environments that are not able to receive what you have to offer. The only part of the process that's personal is your response. Radical self-honesty coupled with neutrality—the perspective that everything is feedback—prevents us from getting discouraged and spinning a story that isn't necessarily true. More often than not, the stories we tell ourselves are based on past experiences rather than present realities. While it's important to make sense of the world, our stories have the potential to tether us to the past and steal a piece of our energy that would rather flow than spin in loops. Inner narratives gain momentum the longer we entertain them. Just five seconds of negative self-talk can take us so far out of our flow that we forget what we're doing and head straight for the bar! Viewing everything as feedback without taking things personally empowers us to navigate life with equanimity and grace.

Feedback brings us back to where we started—Presence. This is how we stay on our upward growth spiral. We express ourselves in Flow, receive feedback in Presence, and integrate the information in Energy Integrity. We then refine our approach and continuously move toward mastery (Transformation), which allows us to flow more… On and on it goes, where you'll end up, nobody knows. Aligned and in flow, life becomes a grand adventure. We don't know where our path will lead and that is by design. *In flow, the process is the outcome*—all we need to do is align with the process.

Reverse Flow Pathway

Like flow, reverse flow gathers momentum over time. However, instead of taking us on an upward growth spiral, reverse flow takes us further and further out of alignment and adds to our backlog of unprocessed energy. The first three stages of reverse flow—distraction, avoidance, and compensation—bring us to the fourth and final stage, which is control. It's human nature to try to control our outer world when our inner world isn't flowing. In reverse flow, instead of receiving feedback and responding accordingly, we adopt a defensive posture and start seeing everything as a threat to our overly controlled inner world. Control becomes a way to preserve inner equilibrium and avoid getting triggered. Despite what may appear as armor of steel, reverse flow leads to mental/emotional fragility and the need to increasingly defend one's reality. At this stage, there's so much unprocessed energy that the slightest offense can trigger an emotional implosion or explosion that lasts for days.

Chasing Energy

At this final stage of reverse flow, one flips from an inside-out orientation that's aligned with nature (receiving and expressing) to an outside-in orientation (chasing and suppressing) that leads to feeling progressively empty on the inside. Life becomes one long chase in an attempt to find what is lost—our own energy and flow. Over time, we forget what it feels like to be still and receive fresh energy from within, so we settle for recycled energy in the form of stress hormones and over-consumption. The solution is always to move back into alignment and reconnect to the energy within. This is often avoided because connecting with oneself brings up all that's been suppressed so that it can be processed and released; however, presence brings fresh energy, and the increased flow naturally flushes out any heaviness we've been carrying.

Projecting Our Light

When we chase and consume energy, rather than receive and express it, our light is suppressed. Anything suppressed becomes a filter through which we see life, which means that whatever we suppress, we project outward. This leads to chasing one's brilliance instead of expressing it, which can take the form of endless trainings, diet and exercise programs, shopping, and more. Instead of moving into presence where our gifts are revealed, we can fall into the trap of thinking that if we only had more money, education, perfection, etc., we'd be happy. The only problem is that there's never enough to fill the hole of reverse flow. *The only way to find our light is to express it.*

It's important to practice compassion for ourselves and anyone stuck in reverse flow as we are living in a world that promotes reverse-flow values. The only way to know that there's another way of being is to put our toe in the river of our own life and see how good it feels. Eventually, we submerge our whole body and choose to live in a state of receptivity and purpose-driven flow. We give to receive and receive to give. Abundant energy wellness is ours when we choose to receive rather than chase, create rather than consume, and connect rather than control.

Leveling Up

The gifts of Flow are *fulfillment* and *purpose*. We are fulfilled each time we give, create, and express from a place of fullness. Purpose is our "why." It's the reason we choose to opt out of stress culture in favor of living in alignment with our own flow. The *Energy Wellness Blueprint* aligns us with our natural flow design, and over time, we develop a flow personality—we become fluid, inspired, and ever-evolving. This inside-out way of being is self-reinforcing; it feels so good that we wouldn't trade it for anything in the world. We balance meaningful activity with periods of renewal and receptivity, a rhythm that sustains our energy and fuels our purpose. For those with a flow personality, presence becomes a habit, integrity is a way of being, and giving and receiving merge into one endless stream of energy that sends ripples of goodness far and wide. Aligned and in our flow, we contribute our special something—our fruit—to the world *and make it better.*

Celebrate Your Flow

What we focus on expands. Reflecting on the times that you flow throughout the day shines a light on these moments and highlights what's working. The feeling of flow is unmistakable, but sometimes it's so subtle that we take it for granted or miss it altogether. I encourage you to take time at the end of each day to write down your flow experiences, big and small. Keep in mind that energy flows through our body at different speeds, and therefore different activities yield different flow experiences. You might experience full-on macro flow while working on a passion project, whereas a walk in the park produces a gentler flow experience. Key macro flow indicators include being completely absorbed in an activity, not thinking of other things, and an altered perception of time—time can fly, slow down, or seem to stop altogether. Micro flow experiences such as a good conversation or focusing on a task typically generate positive feelings such as connection, contentment, joy, and the satisfaction of a job well done. Be generous with your list as you're probably in flow more often than you think!

8

Living in Flow

WHAT DOES ALIGNMENT LOOK LIKE from a practical perspective? This of course depends on the person, but in general, we begin our day connecting within. We fill ourselves up with our own energy *before* venturing out into the world. Filling ourselves up first anchors us in resilience and activates our awareness. Activated awareness allows us to navigate the world with fluidity—we sense and know what's happening within and around us and respond accordingly. This prevents us from becoming stressed, drained, or energetically entangled with others.

If and when our awareness alerts us to mounting stress, we quickly intervene with a few mindful breaths so that we don't fall into a full-on stress spiral. We don't take things personally, and are supported by the emotional resilience that comes with abundant inner flow. Our flowing energy acts as a natural buffer that allows things to bounce off of us rather than getting lodged in. This makes us less likely to take on the energy of others because we can feel what's ours and what's not, whereas being empty inside makes room for other energies to jump right in and make themselves at home.

We naturally gravitate toward others who are high vibe and like to flow with us, but rather than judge those we don't vibe with, we extend kindness along with a silent wave of positivity. Being integrated on the inside, we're no longer fueled by polarization. We see outer division for what it is—a projection of inner division and fragmented energy—which is not our reality. Of course, we have opinions, preferences, and heart-felt desires, but tend to stay away from unproductive power struggles. In flow, we become part of the solution, but it's not all that lofty on the day-to-day because our intention is simply to experience energy wellness and to live a life that flows.

We find that contributing, learning, and problem solving vitalizes rather than depletes us because we have the resources needed to fully engage, and of course, giving back keeps us flowing. That said, after an hour or two of intense concentration, we "take five" to give our brain a break and balance our nervous system. Perhaps we move around, take some mindful breaths, or walk outside to soak in the natural environment. Invariably, we weave in some exercise or gentle movement to promote physical flow and shake off any accumulated stress. Movement, along with other energy wellness practices, becomes a form of daily therapy, keeping us aligned, clear, and open on the inside.

Boundaries take on a new meaning. They are entirely there to protect our energy wellness and flow. This means that we set boundaries a little differently, saying things like, *thank you for thinking of me, but I feel like I need to recharge tonight.* Whereas saying no used to be harder to do, we understand that saying no to one thing means saying yes to showing up as your best self, which ultimately benefits even those we're saying no to. Because we're fueled by purpose-driven flow, we prioritize the activities that light us up. This creates natural boundaries because there's only so much time in a day. That said, in flow, our relationship with time changes. We no longer sit on the side of our river and watch time pass us by. We're living in our flow, which sometimes goes fast and sometimes goes slow.

When an emotion arises within us, we tend to it, knowing that emotion is just energy in motion and what we resist persists. Leaning into our emotions with awareness and neutrality allows us to feel our feelings and receive their gifts (information, integration, and insight). We address our inner world as quickly as we would address a child who needs our attention. This responsiveness keeps us open and flowing. When something arises that's too heavy to process in the moment, we allow it to be there, remaining in alignment (present and aware) without rushing the process. We ask for support when needed, as sometimes all we need is for someone to hold space for us as we try to make sense of things. Sometimes we need others to hold space for a long time and that's okay too.

When we do get stuck, we remind ourselves that we're human and that no one is in perfect flow all of the time. We remember that nature's flow brings turbulence as well as calm, and in fact, those who are most committed to living in organic integrity (aligned with our fundamental nature) often face more challenges than those who are unaware or tend to avoid. And if you feel like you've had more than your fair share of challenges, it's likely because you've decided not to delay the inevitable but instead face things head on like a buffalo walking into a storm because that's the fastest way to move through it. Challenges, even those that persist for a long time, are part of the journey and we can't fast forward our journey. We can certainly delay our growth, but staying present and practicing radical self-honesty prevents challenges from holding on longer than they need to.

Living in alignment, we've entered an upward growth spiral that unfolds the seeds of our greatness and aligns us with our purpose. To support this natural unfolding, we take time each day to reflect on what we did well as well as opportunities for refinement. We do this with zero self-judgment as judgment is a flow blocker. Rather than spin a story, we ask ourselves, how could I have handled this better? If we need to make amends for something, we do so as soon as possible, but often, we just need to make amends with ourselves by taking responsibility for our part coupled with the intention to do better next time.

Perhaps what matters most is the *positive energy* that we bring to others. To be clear, this isn't a flowery type of positivity but a natural outcome of healthy flow. When our energy seamlessly flows and interacts without pretense, others are able to relax in our presence. This creates an open environment that invites authenticity, connection, and interpersonal flow. In flow, we can be positive *and* sad, or positive *and* frustrated. As long as our energy is flowing and we are showing up as our authentic self, we are positive, safe, and uplifting to be around. The emerging research on emotional contagion validates what we already know—our energy impacts others. The ripple effect of your positive presence is so big that it can't be put it into words. It's impossible to know who your energy touches and what gifts it brings. My hunch is that a positive presence brings to others whatever it is that they need in that moment. Somehow, our energy just knows where to flow.

You Are Highly Original

Living in our own flow changes us—first on the inside and then on the outside. We become more and more ourselves, which makes us highly original. We simply can't be anything other than ourselves because trying to be something we're not pulls us out of our flow and depletes our energy. Part of embracing our originality is that everything becomes an act of creativity. In creative flow, we find freedom: the freedom to be exactly as we are and the freedom to contribute to this beautiful world in our own way. As we transform, the world transforms along with us. I can't think of a better time to fully align with your originality, as this is just what the world needs: it needs us to show up energized, inspired, and ready to do our part. Your part might be emanating a positive presence that brings others peace, or it might be inventing a device that saves lives. It all starts within as we receive our own energy in presence, apply it with integrity, and express it with courage. Mistakes are welcome. Challenges are expected. And purpose is guaranteed.

In short, your energy wellness matters. It matters to you and it matters to those who love you. It matters because we're all connected and we need one another to move forward in a way that elevates the whole. This and so much more is possible as we live in alignment with our own flow.

NOTES

NOTES

NOTES

NOTES

NOTES

Acknowledgments

IT'S IMPOSSIBLE TO LIST all the people who've inspired and contributed to this project but I'd like to name a few. I'd like to first thank Luis Medina for introducing me to Adrian Bejan and the constructal law, and for sprinkling his magic dust on this cover design. Luis, your energy is in this project from start to finish!

I'd like to extend a heart-felt thanks to Adrian Bejan, the brilliant mind, courageous disrupter, and father of the constructal law. Thank you Professor Bejan for generously offering your time and support over the past several years. Your impact is massive—good ideas always flow. ☺

I lost both my parents while writing this book. While it's sad beyond words to witness this aspect of organic flow, it cemented a bond with my siblings that carries me and adds stability to what sometimes feels like a wobbly world. Ron, your presence and contribution to The Flow Lab mean more than you know—and is a big reason this book is finally finished! Thank you. Kris, thank you for your presence, friendship, and willingness to edit yet another book. Michelle, your fierceness and unwavering support isn't lost on me—thanks for being a trailblazer and showing us what's possible when you commit to a vision.

Anna, thank you for being a ripple of positivity in my life and in the world. Your brilliance and love is infused in these words, and you demonstrate the law of flow more than anyone I know. Always keep swimming and so will I.

There are many others to thank: my clients who give me as much as I give them (you *know* who you are), my friends who are on this flow journey with me (it wouldn't be the same without you!), and my extended family, who thankfully remain close so we can navigate this life together.

My hope is that this book finds its way to anyone who's ever hit a wall (or a thousand) but refuses to give up. Never give up.

Kimberly Kingsley is a counselor, energy wellness coach, and author of *The Energy Cure: How to Recharge Your Life 30 Seconds at a Time*. She's cofounder of *The Flow Lab*—a company dedicated to promoting energy wellness in the workplace. She lives with her family in Scottsdale, Arizona, and can be reached online at kimberlykingsley.com and theflowlab.co.

www.ingramcontent.com/pod-product-compliance
Lightning Source LLC
Chambersburg PA
CBHW040245010526
44119CB00057B/827